Climbing Art Obstacles in Autism

Teaching Visual-Motor Skills through Visually Structured Art Activities

Karen Loden Talmage, M.Ed.
Contributing Author: Vickie Dobrofsky, OTR/L

TASKS GALORE
PUBLISHING INC.

Table of Contents

Table of Contents (continued)

Acknowledgments

I would like to thank Pat Fennell and Laurie Eckenrode for their confidence and support in making this book possible. I also would like to thank the many teachers and therapists that have trained and shaped me to become the teacher that I am today. Thank you Vickie Dobrofsky for always having the answer to everything. Also, thank you for your dedication, offering your expertise and assistance, wherever and whenever they were needed. To my many phenomenal teaching assistants, I want to acknowledge I could not have been the teacher I am without their dedication and support. I want to personally thank each of them, Amy, Paula, Jamie, Kristy, Stephanie, Mary, Clovia, Vickie, Jennie, Becky, Brad, Trish, and, of course, Mona. Her art lives on.

For their various contributions, thanks are extended to David Kennebeck, Mike Morrell, and Belton Chappell.

Special thanks go to my family, Marty and Lynda Loden, who were able to technically and patiently guide me through the process of producing a book. I also want to thank my children Will, Molly, Aline, John, Kate, and Lacy, who have given me everything a mother could ever want. I especially offer many, many thanks to Kate for her patient hand and foot modeling. And thanks go to my husband Bobby, who always has envisioned me writing. His encouragement was the catalyst that helped me approach Tasks Galore about publishing my work.

Finally, this book is dedicated to my many students, past, present, and future. As John Whitehead writes, "Children are the living messages we send to a time we will not see."

Karen Loden Talmage

About the Author

Karen Loden Talmage graduated from Furman University in Greenville, South Carolina with a master's degree in preschool special education. She has taught in the field of special education for seventeen years, many of those years were in preschool special education. After teaching students with orthopedic disabilities for eleven years, Karen received training through Division TEACCH (Treatment and Education of Autistic and related Communication-handicapped Children) and began teaching students with autism spectrum disorders. Karen integrates many aspects of therapy into her daily classroom program in Georgia. This book is a reflection of her commitment to meet her students where they are and to guide them into what they may become.

About the Contributing Author

Vickie Dobrofsky graduated from the University of Kansas with a bachelor's of science degree in occupational therapy. She has more than twenty years of pediatric occupational therapy experience in both clinical and school-based settings in Florida and Georgia. Vickie's recent experiences include providing integrated occupational therapy services to children with autism spectrum disorders. She has a wonderful rapport with both students and teachers and finds working with students with ASD to be personally rewarding. Her insights, coupled with her therapeutic expertise, make her a valuable asset to the preschool special education classroom. She and Karen have worked with each other for the past four years.

"You must plant the seed before you can harvest the crop."
- Unknown

Introduction

Each organization writes its defining characteristics of autism as a complex developmental disability with an emphasis on the prevalent lack of social and communication skills. Admittedly, autism is described as a spectrum with a wide variety of individualized combinations that range from mild to severe. However, few describe the visual-motor difficulties often associated with the autism spectrum disorder (ASD).

With the dramatic rise in diagnosed cases of autism, the disorder has become more prevalent than many other specific disabilities. Teachers and therapists presently carry caseloads of one or more students with ASD. With autism's many facets, it can be difficult to create the perfect singular recipe for an entire disability for purposes of intervention

As a teacher of young students with ASD, I have discovered that the visual structure modeled after Division TEACCH at the University of North Carolina employs successful principles that I apply to a majority of my teaching methods. With respect to childhood art, verbal instructions easily can convert into a sequence of pictured steps to complete a typical early learner art activity. Where art is concerned, I observe that the students begin to realize they can work within visual systems to improve skills and, in turn, understand how their creation could parlay into a form of expressive communication. As first learners, they feel comfort with the visual directions and begin to overcome the anxiety of using their hands and associated tools, such as writing or cutting instruments. The visual systems foster early independence with art materials and enable the student to mount the barriers of visual-motor skills to foster their confidence and creative talent. Our students with autism have the remarkable ability to translate what they see into what they will choose to do. To possess incredible visual spatial skills and, yet, to be unable in the youngest years to translate that into a visual-motor reaction is indeed frustrating to both the child and adult. In using the visual systems for art, where there were once refusals to hold a marker or scissors, there is now an attempt to replicate the visual representation. Using this methodology, teachers and therapists will observe a quick acceptance of the student to enter art activities revolving around precise art tools. This, in turn, accomplishes many individualized objectives found in our student's education or therapy plans, as well as creates typical young art that can be found in the hallways of any elementary school.

The teacher or therapist initiates these activities so that the student develops the visual-motor skills necessary to find art activities pleasurable and self-fulfilling. Yet, ever respectful of the artistic integrity of the student, plenty of opportunities for creative expression must exist beyond adult initiatives. Art will promote an opportunity to express feelings that typically are unheard. The creation of art, whether it is visual, musical, or movement, utilizes unique portions of our brains, especially the brains of a developing child.

This book is intended to provide assistance to teachers, therapists, and, ultimately, the child in obtaining the necessary skills to accomplish the beginning steps to art. It is not solely intended for students with autism but for any student who would gain skills through the use of visual instructions. This is a proven and effective method of instruction for working with students with various learning needs.

It has been amazing to watch students with various disabilities translate the visual directions and independently produce an art product. Without solely relying on the verbal or physical prompts of the teacher or therapist, these students become more productive by fluently and independently interpreting visual directions. Simply stated, the visual structure provided by the photographs aids the verbal prompts that many of our young students do not understand. The sequential nature of the photographs depicts a course of events, including a natural conclusion that can be problematic in the educational or therapeutic environment.

As most teachers and therapists are aware, it is important to create an environment where visual-motor skills are not splintered from their natural occurrences, and the process can become a product. Furthermore, I hope you will develop confidence in your students such that they willingly enter art requiring visual-motor skills. Most importantly, it is critical that the activities remain developmentally appropriate. Many of the selected activities were developed throughout the years as activities that would compliment thematic instruction, and the activities also represent art activities found in typical early classrooms or the specific interests of my students.

Many of us that work with young children have cute stories to share at the end of the day. I love to repeat the stories of how my students approach their individual schedules when they know that the art area is depicted. Many students skip or run to their schedules to arrive as quickly as possible to the art area. Other students glance over to the art area to determine how exciting or messy the project may be, while others immediately gravitate to the visual art directions to figure out what is expected of them in the context of the activity. I guess it is all in how you look at it.

Best wishes in planting the seeds that will one day become the crop,

Karen Loden Talmage

Therapeutic Applications of Visually Structured Art

Children with autism present challenging problems, including sensory processing and modulation difficulties, fine motor deficits, and significant visual-motor delays. Therapy plans are developed to provide the experiences that these children need to mature, but conveying directions can be difficult, and engaging the child in such activities can be met with noncompliant behaviors and inappropriate use of materials. This creates even a greater challenge for the therapist to provide needed intervention.

As an occupational therapist working within the highly structured environment of a classroom for children with ASD, I initially had many doubts as to whether I could deliver effective therapy in such an atmosphere. I quickly learned that those same structures and strategies that I felt might limit my ability to provide intervention were critical to engaging these children in desired activities and in promoting their acquisition of skills.

The visually structured art activities presented in this book have proven to be a powerful and effective avenue for implementation of a therapy program. As will be discussed later, these activities provide opportunities to successfully engage children in tactile sensory experiences, improve fine motor planning, develop upper extremity control and hand skills, develop the ability to manipulate objects and tools, and develop visual-motor skills within a context that is appealing and purposeful for the young child. Although occupational therapists have long recognized the usefulness of art and craft activities for skill development, it is the clear visual presentation of the directions and the visual structure of presented materials that make these activities unique. The sequential pictures initially attract the child's interest, clearly communicate step-by-step instruction, and promote the child's persistence until the task is completed. Therapists will discover that when given a visual format to communicate motor expectations, children with ASD, as well as other visual learners, will engage in presented activities with greater ease and often will demonstrate abilities that one did not even know they possessed!

Although tactile activities typically are offered in an effort to remediate tactile processing problems, children often are not amenable to engaging in those activities. Several tasks have been included that involve painting and printing of the hands or feet to create an image on paper that will become the basis of the art project, for example, "Spider." These tasks require toleration for the textures of the paintbrush and paint on the skin as well as adequate weight bearing or pressure to make the "print." Other activities, like "Ice Cream Cone" and "Snowman Fun," involve messy medians, such as a shaving cream and glue mixture, to spread within a designated boundary and the handling of uncommon objects and textures, such as feathers, cotton, gritty salt, and wax paper, necessary in other projects.

The visual directions provided for these tasks prepare the child for such experiences and define the purpose of doing so. They grade the sensory experience, lending structure and organization to what the child might perceive as aversive and threatening. Time and again, it has been amazing to watch tactilely defensive children delve into a visually structured art activity that requires their hands getting messy without refusing, without tears, and without a willful attempt to run and wash their hands as soon as they come in contact with the materials.

Motivated to successfully complete a visually presented art task, many children, who would be reluctant to accept needed physical assistance and guidance, have been willing to do so.

We sometimes work with children who are quite the opposite of tactilely defensive. They are "sensory seekers" who cannot seem to get enough input and, if offered finger paint to use with their hands, they suddenly have it smeared up their arms and on their faces. The visual cues offered will assist these children as well, defining the limitations of how and where the medium is to be manipulated so that they might more appropriately use such materials.

Engaging children in visually structured art activities on a frequent basis has contributed to significant improvement in the fine motor planning skills of even the most awkward and disorganized. The sequential pictures, paired with visually structured materials, have a strong organizing effect. They break each activity into manageable parts; define what, when, and how objects and materials are to be used to complete the task; and offer a constant visual model that can be referenced during the activity. When children understand the expectation, their ability to initiate participation improves, and their actions become more purposeful. Impulsive behaviors, such as grabbing for presented materials within reach or inappropriate use of items, such as painting or scribbling with a crayon on any available surface, typically are reduced. These art activities provide numerous opportunities to work on components of motor planning, including initiation and the grading of movement and force. Tasks prompt children to grade the size and pressure of their movements to paint or color within a designated area; apply glue on a small dot, rather than create a giant puddle; press downward to squish paint between folded paper; and use tools, such as a stamp pad, hole punch, or stapler. The repetition of similar skills within many tasks helps build competency, but the different applications and combinations of skills required to complete each task will provide enough variation to subtly challenge the child's fine motor planning abilities and, thus, facilitate growth. The activities also will provide opportunity to integrate or generalize specific skills the children might be working on in other aspects of their educational or therapy plan.

Children with ASD and other developmental delays often exhibit deficits in muscle tone, strength, and development of arm-hand patterns essential to the accomplishment of functional activities. Through the performance of embedded skills, the use of specific objects and materials, and attention to visual cues relating to arm-hand use within each activity, a broad range of such foundational issues can be addressed. Opportunities exist for development or improvement of accurate reach skills, crossing the midline of the body, upper extremity strengthening, bilateral hand usage, controlled grasp and release, and tool usage. Careful consideration should always be given to appropriate positioning. Children require a stable base of support and a work surface of appropriate height to best perform fine motor activities. The midline of their activity should align with the midline of their body. Controlled, accurate reach from the shoulder or elbow and crossing of the midline of the body with the hands can readily be facilitated through several activities. Tasks, such as "Airplane," require reach and placement of project pieces in all quadrants of the page. "Feather Painting" is an example that requires painting in all quadrants. "Ant Hill" is an example of printing in a horizontal progression across the page. Thoughtful placement of materials to be accessed can facilitate a wider range of movement beyond the perimeters of the project itself (i.e., to the front, left, or right) and more frequent opportunities to cross midline.

Working with the arm in the extended position away from the body, as required to spray water on a vertical surface, and manipulation of resistive objects, such as a spray bottle in the activity "Rain"; squeezing glue bottles with the finger tips and tearing stiff paper into pieces as found in "Spring Flower"; operating a stapler while completing "Ant Hat"; using a hole punch for the activity "Bird"; manipulating small brads used for the activities "Alligator" and "Ladybug"; and opening small paint containers that are used with "Airplane," "Feather Painting," and "Kite" all contribute to strengthening the muscles of the shoulders, arms, and hands. Bilateral hand usage, particularly the ability to use the hands in a dominant/assistor fashion, is a clear component of these art activities.

The photographs indicate the use of one hand for stabilization or holding of an object, while the other is performing an action during all drawing, painting, gluing, and cutting tasks. This often is not spontaneous and must be prompted in young children so that they can manage fine motor tasks with greater independence and improved control. "Heart Bracelet," a stringing task, offers experience with bilateral manipulation. The ability to isolate fingers to perform a portion of the activity is emphasized in "Ant Hill," "Apple Basket," and "Humpty Dumpty." The use of refined grasp patterns are promoted as children manipulate small two-or three-dimensional parts of tasks, including brads, wiggle eyes, pom-poms, cotton balls, sequins, pipe cleaners, animal crackers, and paper shapes. All activities involving coloring and drawing clearly picture the ulnar (small finger) side of the hand stabilized on the table surface, the wrist stabilized in extension, and use of a mature tripod grasp for holding crayons. Cutting tasks picture the forearm in a neutral posture and scissors correctly positioned in the hand. Such visual cues can be used to assist development of these desired patterns.

It is important for young children to attain competency with the use of tools such as scissors, paintbrushes, and crayons. Ability to effectively grasp and control movement of these tools provides a strong foundation for the development of their visual-motor skills. For example, learning to correctly hold and manipulate scissors using the thumb, first, and middle fingers encourages hand development related to efficient pencil grasp and the ability to produce simple straight and curved lines is the basis of letter formation. Acquisition of such skills can be fostered naturally as children attempt cutting projects and embellish their creations with crayon strokes. The wide range of embedded cutting and prewriting skills offered within these art activities are outlined below:

Cutting Skills
Snipping: Heart Bracelet
Cutting with forward progression on a short straight line: Firetruck, Kite, Lion
Cutting with forward progression on a long straight line: Ant Hat, Bee, Bird Nest, Handprint Flower, Jellyfish, Ladybug, Zoo
Cutting straight line forms: House, Ice Cream Cone, S'more, Train, Dinosaur, Humpty Dumpty, Tractor
Cutting on a curved line: Watermelon, Apple Basket
Cutting curved line forms: Bear, Bird Print, Penguin, Pizza, Polar Bear, Snowman, Dinosaur, Humpty Dumpty, and Tractor

Prewriting Skills

Producing vertical strokes: House, Tractor, Umbrella, Zebra

Producing horizontal strokes: House, Train

Producing diagonal strokes: Alligator, Barn, Chicken

Producing curved lines: Apple Basket, Bear, Butterfly Footprint, Dinosaur, Humpty Dumpty, Jellyfish, Lion, Polar Bear, Snowman, and Umbrella

Producing large and small circles: Airplane, Bear, Bee, Bird Print, Butterfly Footprint, Chicken, Dinosaur, Giraffe, Humpty Dumpty, and Tractor

It should be noted that the photographs visually will prompt children to produce specific forms, but, until they develop reliable skills in this area, they often will produce dots, small scribble marks, and straight lines within their capabilities. These deliberate efforts are perfectly acceptable, if not exciting, when working with some children.

The tasks presented in this book are multi-faceted, typically offering the opportunity to work on several skills or providing intervention in several deficit areas. However, the author's careful step-by-step analysis of each task readily lends itself to simplication. When necessary, each task can be modified, and specific components targeted to adapt it for any level. Using the same activity, one child may work toward independent performance of a four-step task, while another works toward maintaining grasp of a tool for ten seconds. The level of support offered can be adjusted to meet individual needs. Higher functioning children might be expected to secure materials and proceed through a task independently, while others require supervision or additional prompting to reference pictures and move through the task. Lower functioning children may need physical guidance to perform certain steps. Structure can be increased by reducing the amount of information presented (i.e., one picture at a time), offering only those materials required to complete each step, or providing additional visual supports. Reduction of steps and preparation of materials to decrease the number of repetitions or the difficulty of a particular skill effectively can decrease the workload. The following example of a cut and paste task illustrates this: cutting steps can be eliminated by providing pre-cut pieces and allowing the child to proceed to gluing and placing materials, and repetitions of cutting on a six inch straight line can be reduced to a snip. Through such simple modifications, these activities have been used successfully with children exhibiting a wide range of intellectual functioning and varied disabilities in both educational and clinical settings.

Vickie Dobrofsky

Implementation

With many of our young learners having unique learning needs, the process of guiding the learner from one activity to another can be an obstacle to performance. When the learner makes the transition to an art activity, it is helpful to employ the same visual structure as found within the activity itself.

The visual method chosen for the students' transition to the art area is dependent on their understanding. When a student is dependent on objects to interpret meaning, an instructor can guide the student to the art area with an object that represents the activity. For example, the instructor may hand students a paintbrush, crayon, or glue in order to have them proceed to the art area. The student then could use the object to initiate the project, or it might mean that the student would color on a blank sheet of paper for about one minute prior to beginning the scheduled structured art activity. Such a transition gives the student information concerning what will be occurring next, often a problematic situation for our learners with anxiety about that, as well as offers a concrete method of terminating one activity so that another activity can begin. For a student who is beginning to move away from object level, an instructor may hand the student a schedule card on which an object related to art has been attached. The student then would move to the art area with the card and put it in a designated place prior to beginning the activity. Many of our students have moved beyond the concrete transitions of objects and are able to interpret photographs and line drawings and, subsequently, already are employing personal schedules. When such students are cued to check their schedules, a picture of the art area would indicate to the students that they will be moving to art as their next scheduled activity. The student removes the art area picture from his or her schedule, moves to the area, and places the art picture in a designated spot. When our students are able to read, personal schedules using written words may indicate that the activity of art is next and the student will, in turn, move to the art area.

An instructor hands a student a physical cue to indicate that she is to check her schedule in order to move to the upcoming art activity.

This is an example of a schedule card with an object attached that could be used to move the student to the art area.

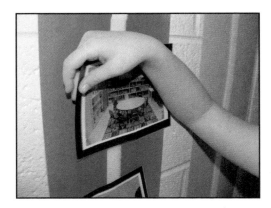

The student removes an image that indicates she should move to the art area next.

If the student is working directly with an instructor, he or she determines how to implement the visual instructions in this book, as well as the art supplies. If the student is completing art activities independently, the student arrives at the art area, and the visual instructions, found in this book, as well as the required art supplies, could be located in a basket so that the student will have all necessary materials to begin the art activity. For a higher level learner, the student may arrive at a designated area and collect necessary art materials from readily marked and organized locations, using both the list of necessary supplies and the picture of necessary supplies from the activity pages found in this book.

While at the art area, the instructor might employ additional visual cues to assist performance. The instructor may use photographs or symbols to remind the student of required behaviors, such as "quiet," "paint on paper," or "glue on dots." The physical boundaries of the art area need to be clearly defined to assist the students in knowing where they should position to complete the activities. For example, footprints can be placed on the floor to give visual information as to where to stand if the student is to stand while completing any of the activities.

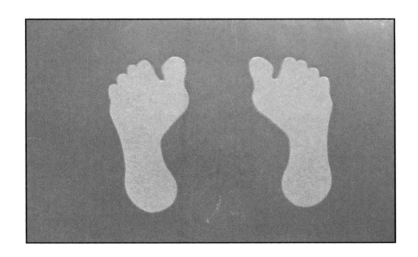

This is an example of footprints that the instructor strategically can place where he or she would like the student to remain during art instruction. This provides ultimate visual structure that may be needed if the student has difficulties remaining in a designated area while working with messy art materials.

Airplane

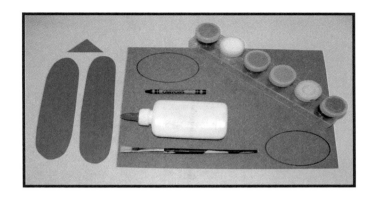

Airplane Supplies:

- ☐ two red ovals
- ☐ red triangle
- ☐ blue paper
- ☐ black crayon
- ☐ glue
- ☐ paintbrush
- ☐ paint set

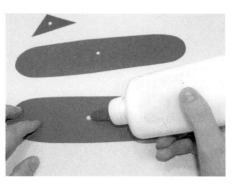

1. Put glue on dots.

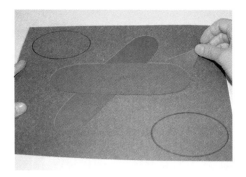

2. Put airplane on paper.

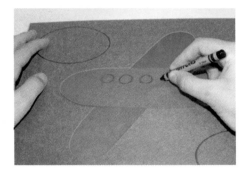

3. Draw circles for airplane windows.

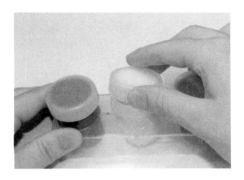

4. Take lid off white paint.

5. Paint clouds.

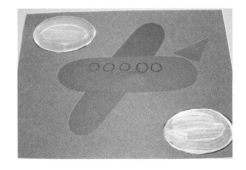

6. Your airplane is ready to fly!

Alligator

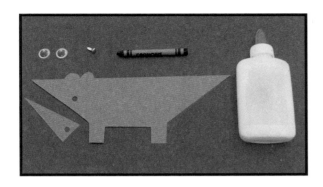

Alligator Supplies:

- ☐ alligator
- ☐ alligator jaw
- ☐ black crayon
- ☐ brad
- ☐ two wiggle eyes
- ☐ glue

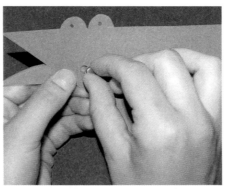

1. Push brad through holes and fasten.

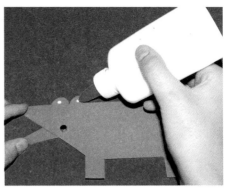

2. Put glue on dots.

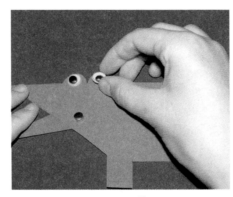

3. Put eyes on glue.

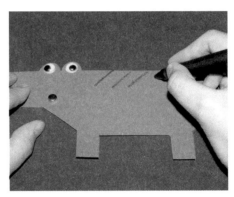

4. Draw alligator ridges.

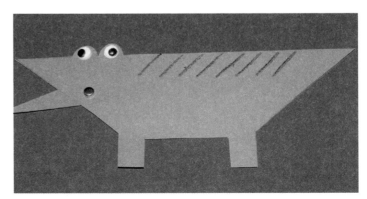

5. Is your alligator going to the swamp?

Ant Hat

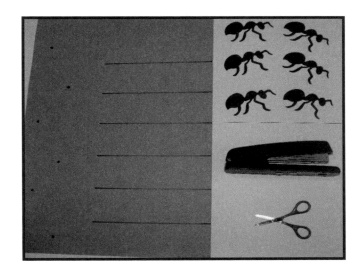

Ant Hat Supplies:

☐ green paper

☐ ants

☐ stapler

☐ scissors

☐ glue

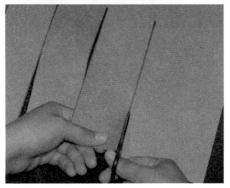

1. Cut lines on green paper.

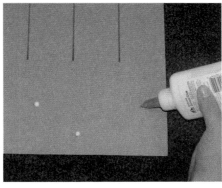

2. Put glue on dots.

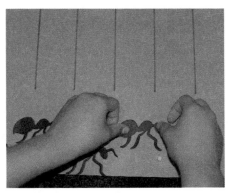

3. Put ants on glue.

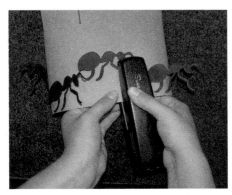

4. Staple the hat together.

5. Now, you can wear your ant hat!

Ant Hill

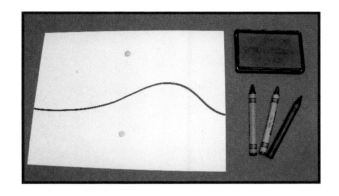

Ant Hill Supplies:

☐ blue crayon

☐ brown crayon

☐ black crayon

☐ red ink pad

☐ white paper

1. Push thumb onto red ink pad.

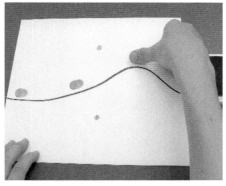

2. Push thumb onto hill on white paper.

3. Draw legs on ants.

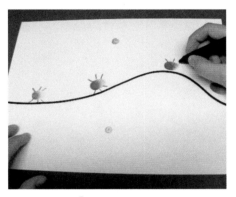

4. Color the ground brown.

5. Color the sky blue.

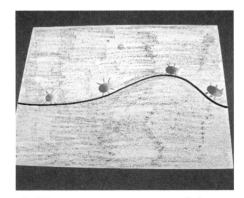

6. Your ants are working hard!

Apple Basket

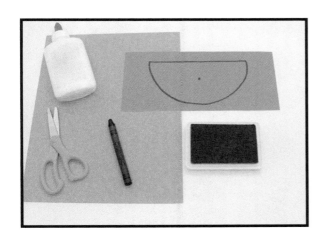

Apple Basket Supplies:

- ☐ green paper
- ☐ scissors
- ☐ brown semi-circle
- ☐ red ink pad
- ☐ black crayon
- ☐ glue

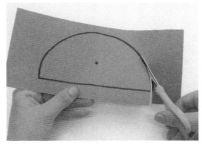

1. Cut brown basket.

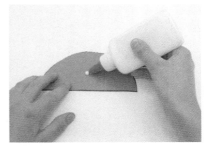

2. Put glue on basket.

3. Put basket on paper.

4. Draw a handle.

5. Push your thumb onto the ink pad.

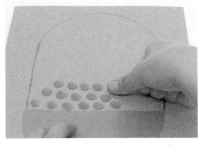

6. Push your thumb into the basket.

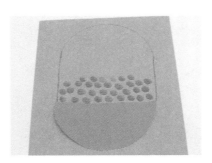

7. A tisket, a tasket, a little brown basket!

15

Barn

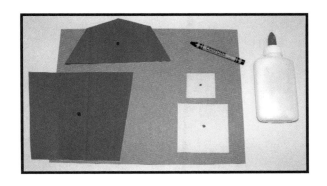

Barn Supplies:

- [ ] green paper
- [ ] red barn roof
- [ ] red barn
- [ ] small yellow square
- [ ] big yellow square
- [ ] black crayon
- [ ] glue

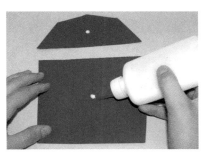

1. Put glue on dots.

2. Put barn on green paper.

3. Draw lines on barn.

4. Put glue on barn doors.

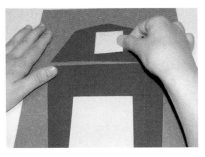

5. Put doors on barn.

6. Draw X's on barn doors.

7. Your barn is finished!

Bear

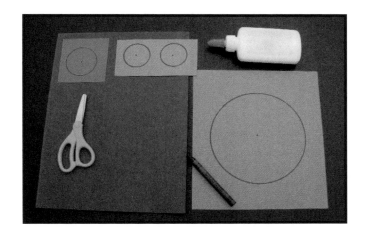

Bear Supplies:

- [ ] black paper
- [ ] big brown circle
- [ ] red circle
- [ ] two small brown circles
- [ ] scissors
- [ ] black crayon
- [ ] glue

1. Cut big brown circle.

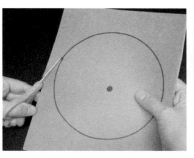

2. Cut red circle.

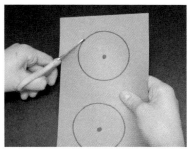

3. Cut two brown circles.

4. Put glue on dots.

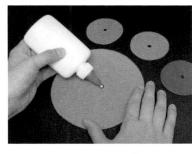

5. Put big brown circle on black paper.

6. Put two brown ears on the bear head.

7. Put red circle on the bear face.

8. Draw eyes and mouth on the bear.

9. Did you know bears have shaggy fur and a short tail?

Bee

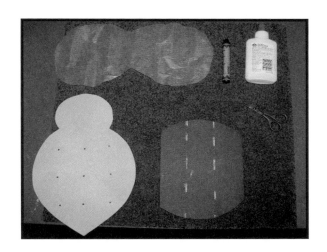

Bee Supplies:

☐ yellow bee body

☐ wax paper wings

☐ black paper

☐ black crayon

☐ glue

☐ scissors

1. Put glue on dots on one side of the bee.

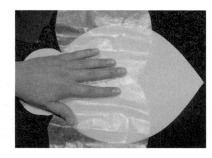

2. Put wings on the bee.

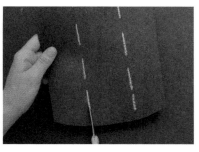

3. Cut black stripes.

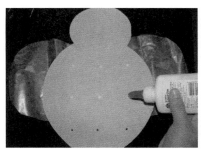

4. Put glue on dots on the other side of bee.

5. Put stripes on the bee.

6. Draw eyes on your bee.

7. Your bee is finished!

Bird

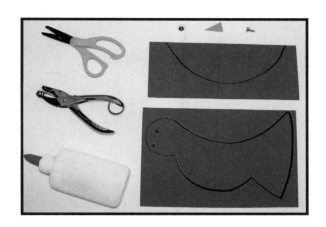

Bird Supplies:

- [ ] red bird body
- [ ] red wing
- [ ] scissors
- [ ] hole punch
- [ ] glue
- [ ] wiggle eye
- [ ] orange beak
- [ ] brad

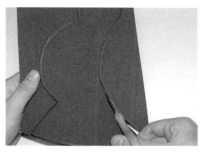

1. Cut bird body.

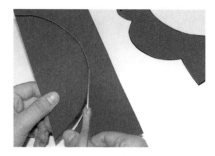

2. Cut bird wing.

3. Hole punch the wing and body.

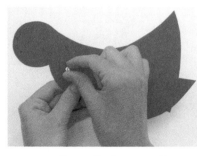

4. Put brad through the holes and fasten.

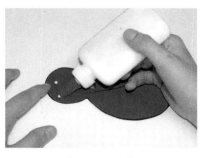

5. Put glue on dots.

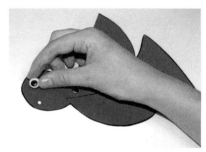

6. Put eye on the bird.

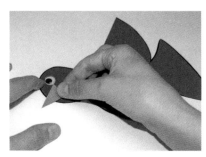

7. Put beak on the bird.

8. Fly bird! Fly!

Bird Nest

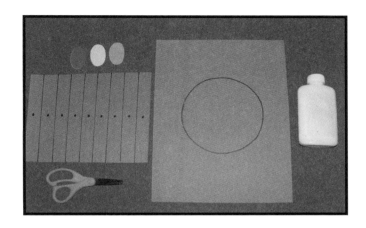

Bird Nest Supplies:

- [ ] green paper
- [ ] three bird eggs
- [ ] brown striped paper
- [ ] scissors
- [ ] glue

1. Cut brown strips.

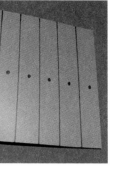

2. Put glue on dots.

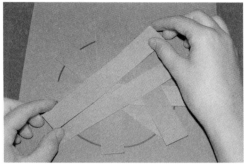

3. Put brown strips on circle.

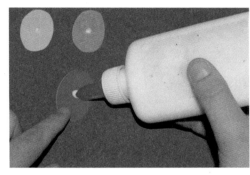

4. Put glue on dots.

5. Put eggs into nest.

6. Your bird nest is finished!

Bird Print

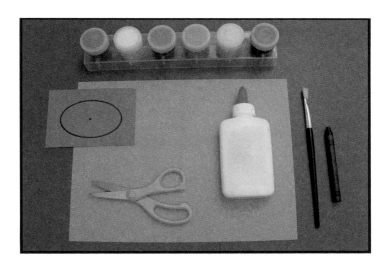

Bird Handprint Supplies:

- [ ] blue paper
- [ ] paint set
- [ ] paintbrush
- [ ] blue oval
- [ ] black crayon
- [ ] scissors
- [ ] glue

1. Cut blue oval.

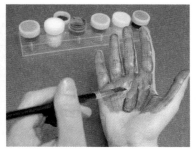

2. Paint both of your hands blue.

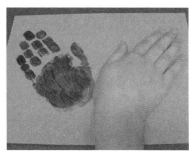

3. Push your hands onto the blue paper.

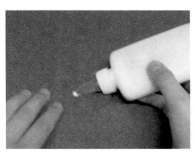

4. Put glue on dot.

5. Put blue oval in between handprints.

6. Draw eyes.

7. This is your bird handprint!

8. Wash your dirty hands in a sink.

Butterfly Footprint

Butterfly Footprint Supplies:

- ☐ blue paper
- ☐ yellow butterfly body
- ☐ black crayon
- ☐ paintbrush and paint set
- ☐ washcloth
- ☐ glue

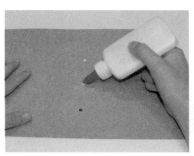

1. Put glue on dots.

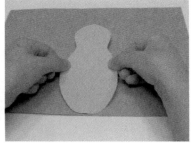

2. Put body on blue paper.

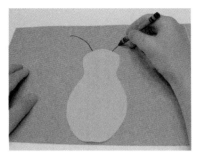

3. Draw antennae on the head.

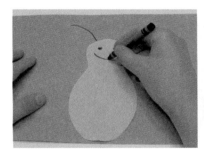

4. Draw a face on the butterfly.

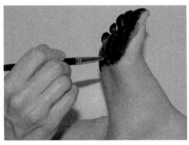

5. Paint your feet black.

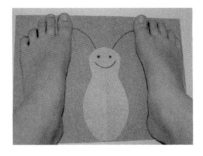

6. Step onto the blue paper.

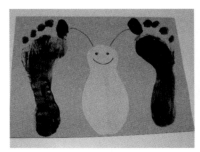

7. Your butterfly footprint is finished!

8. Wash your feet.

Caterpillar

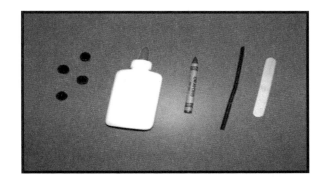

Caterpillar Supplies:

- [ ] four brown pom-poms
- [ ] glue
- [ ] brown crayon
- [ ] brown pipe cleaner
- [ ] craft stick

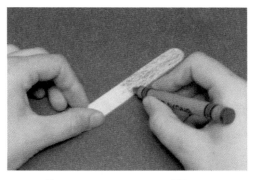

1. Color your caterpillar stick.

2. Twist the pipe cleaner around the stick.

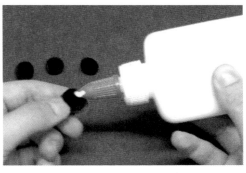

3. Put glue on pom-poms.

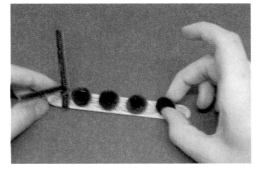

4. Put pom-poms on the caterpillar.

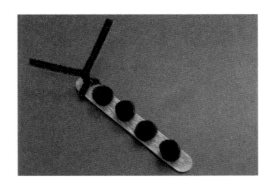

5. Your caterpillar is ready to make a cocoon!

Chicken

Chicken Supplies:

- [ ] glue
- [ ] yellow paint
- [ ] paintbrush
- [ ] white paper
- [ ] orange and black crayons
- [ ] yellow feather

1. Draw a circle.

2. Draw a small circle on top of the circle.

3. Draw lines for the chicken legs.

4. Paint the chicken.

5. Put glue on the chicken.

6. Draw a beak on the chicken.

7. Put the feather on the glue.

8. Your chicken is ready to eat corn!

Cloud

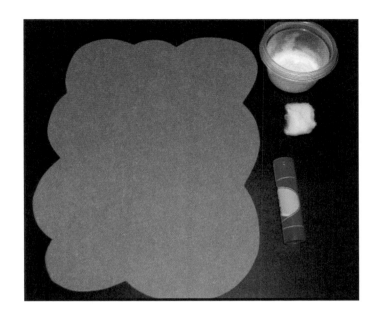

Cloud Supplies:

- [ ] blue paper
- [ ] baby powder
- [ ] cotton ball
- [ ] glue stick

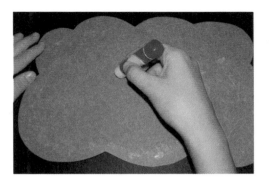

1. Put glue on all of the blue paper.

2. Put baby powder on the cloud.

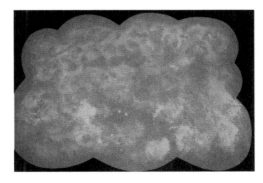

3. A cloud has many water droplets inside it.

Dinosaur

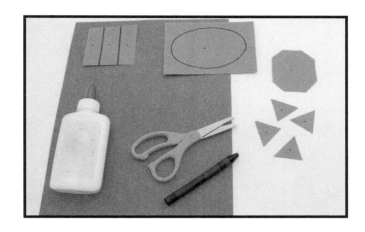

Dinosaur Supplies:

- [ ] glue
- [ ] scissors
- [ ] black crayon
- [ ] dinosaur body parts
- [ ] green paper

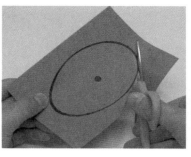

1. Cut brown oval.

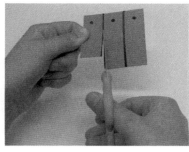

2. Cut brown rectangles.

3. Put glue on dots.

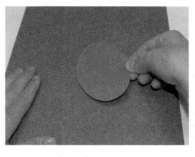

4. Put body on paper.

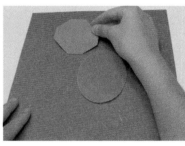

5. Put head on body.

6. Put arm and legs on body.

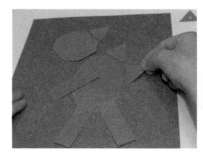

7. Put spines on body.

8. Draw an eye and mouth on the head.

9. This is your finished dinosaur!

Feather Painting

Feather Painting Supplies:

☐ paint set

☐ six colored feathers

☐ white paper with circles

1. Take tops off paint set.

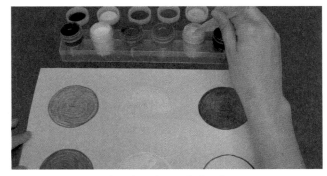

2. Paint each circle with the matching colored feather.

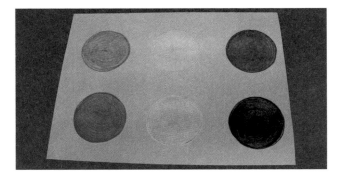

3. This is your finished painting. You did a good job of matching colors!

Firetruck

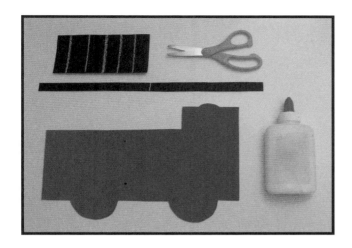

Firetruck Supplies:

☐ red fire truck

☐ black striped paper

☐ long black paper strip

☐ scissors

☐ glue

1. Cut black paper strips on lines.

2. Put glue on dots.

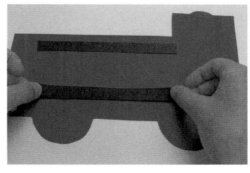

3. Put ladder on firetruck.

4. Put glue on ladder rungs.

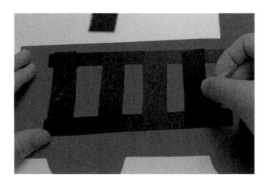

5. Put ladder rungs on the firetruck.

6. Ready for a fire!

Fishbowl

Fishbowl Supplies:

☐ blue paint

☐ salt

☐ white paper with a blue circle

☐ paintbrush

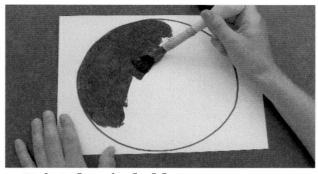

1. Paint the circle blue.

2. Sprinkle the blue circle with salt.

3. This is your finished painting. It will shine when it is dry.

Fish in a Bowl

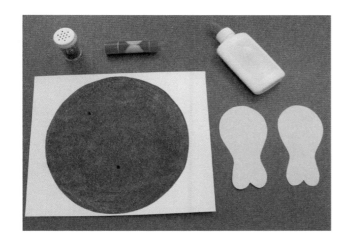

Fish in a Bowl Supplies:

- ☐ fish bowl
- ☐ glitter
- ☐ glue stick
- ☐ glue
- ☐ two fish

1. Use gluestick and put glue on fish.

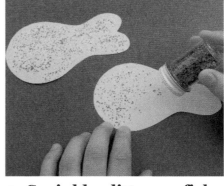

2. Sprinkle glitter on fish.

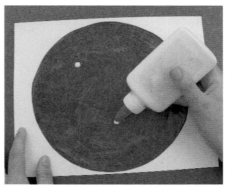

3. Put glue on dots.

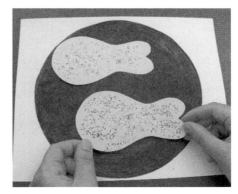

4. Put fish on glue.

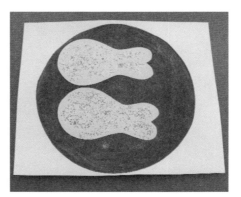

5. This is your finished fish in a fishbowl!

Ghost

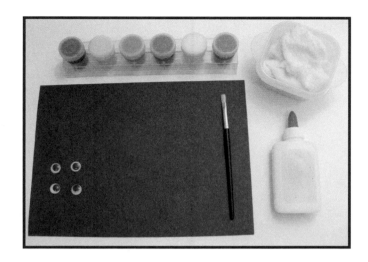

Ghost Supplies:

- ☐ paint set
- ☐ black paper
- ☐ paintbrush
- ☐ washcloth
- ☐ two wiggle eyes
- ☐ glue

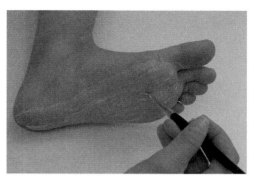

1. Paint your feet white.

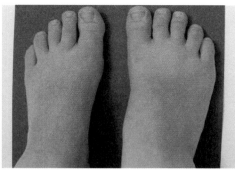

2. Step on your black paper.

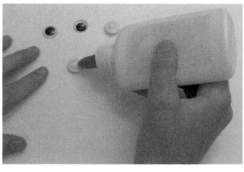

3. Put glue on the back of the wiggle eyes.

4. Put wiggle eyes on ghosts.

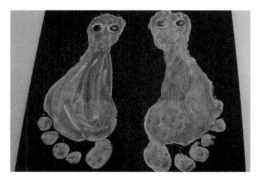

5. BOO! Your ghosts are scary!

6. Wash your feet.

Giraffe

Giraffe Supplies:

☐ yellow giraffe

☐ wiggle eye

☐ brown crayon

☐ glue

1. Color brown spots on your giraffe.

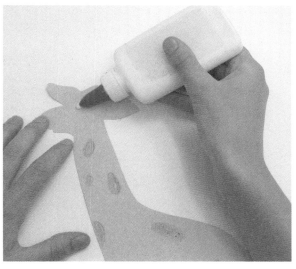

2. Put glue on dot.

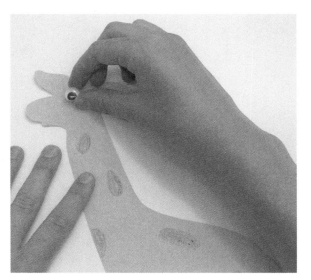

3. Put wiggle eye on glue.

4. This is your finished giraffe!

Handprint Flower

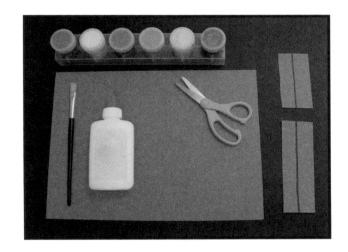

Handprint Flower Supplies:

- [ ] blue paper
- [ ] paint set and paintbrush
- [ ] scissors
- [ ] long green paper strip
- [ ] short green paper strip
- [ ] glue

1. Cut two green paper strips.

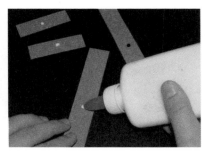

2. Put glue on dots.

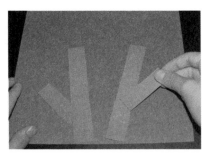

3. Put green stems and leaves on blue paper.

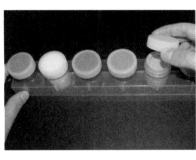

4. Take top off yellow paint.

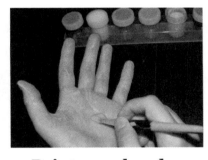

5. Paint your hands yellow.

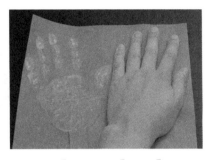

6. Push your hands onto the blue paper.

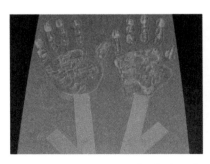

7. This is your finished flower handprint!

8. Wash your hands.

Heart Bracelet

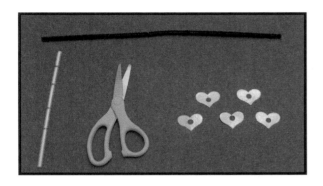

Heart Bracelet Supplies:

- [ ] pipe cleaner
- [ ] drinking straw
- [ ] five hearts
- [ ] scissors

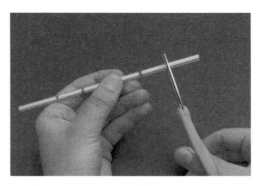

1. Cut straw on lines.

2. Push straw through pipe cleaner.

3. Push heart through pipe cleaner. Continue the pattern.

4. Twist ends of pipe cleaner.

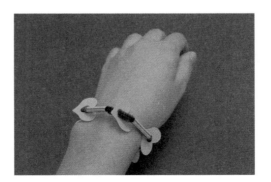

5. You can wear your heart bracelet!

House

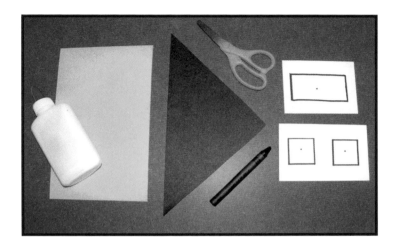

House Supplies:

- [ ] yellow rectangle
- [ ] black triangle
- [ ] glue
- [ ] black crayon
- [ ] scissors
- [ ] white rectangle
- [ ] two white squares

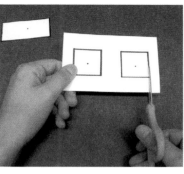

1. Cut white squares and rectangle.

2. Put glue on dots.

3. Put the door on the house.

4. Put the windows on the house.

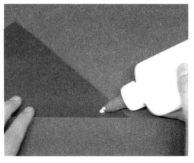

5. Put glue on the roof.

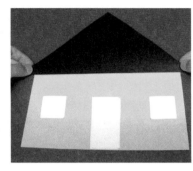

6. Put the roof on the house.

7. Draw crosses in the windows.

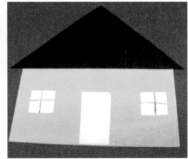

8. This is the finished house!

Humpty Dumpty

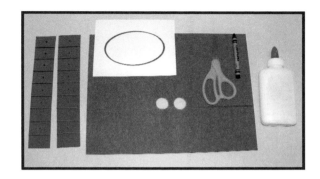

Humpty Dumpty Supplies:

- ☐ red paper strips
- ☐ white oval
- ☐ blue paper
- ☐ scissors
- ☐ black crayon
- ☐ glue

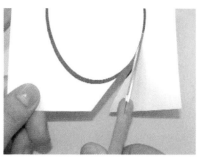

1. Cut white oval.

2. Cut red rectangles.

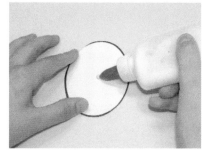

3. Put glue on dot.

4. Put glue on dots.

5. Put head on blue paper.

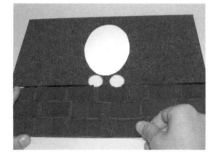

6. Put bricks on blue paper.

7. Draw Humpty's face.

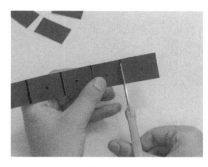

8. Stick your fingers through the holes and wiggle your fingers!

Ice Cream Cone

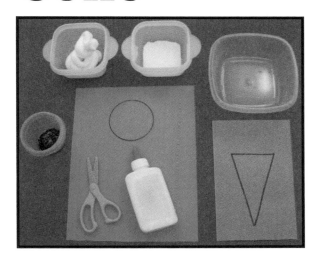

Ice Cream Cone Supplies:

- ☐ brown triangle
- ☐ pink paper
- ☐ shaving cream
- ☐ scissors
- ☐ empty container
- ☐ sprinkles
- ☐ glue

1. Cut triangle.

2. Put glue on dot.

3. Put cone under circle on pink paper.

4. Mix shaving cream and glue.

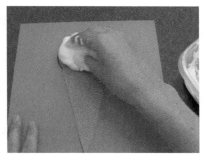

5. Put mixture on circle on pink paper.

6. Put sprinkles on top of the mixture.

7. This is your finished ice cream cone!

8. Wash your hands.

Jellyfish

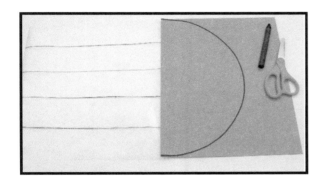

Jellyfish Supplies:

- [ ] blue paper
- [ ] lined wax paper attached to blue paper
- [ ] black crayon
- [ ] scissors

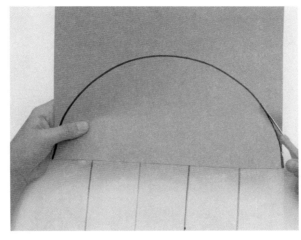

1. Cut jellyfish body.

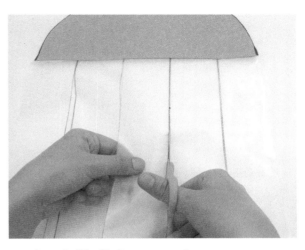

2. Cut jellyfish tentacles.

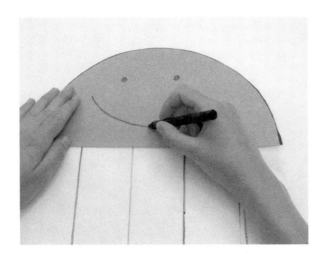

3. Draw a face on the jellyfish.

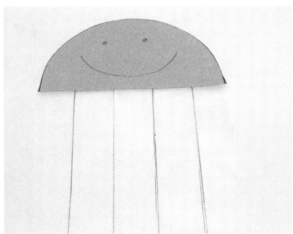

4. A jellyfish can sting you with its long tentacles. Watch out!

Kite

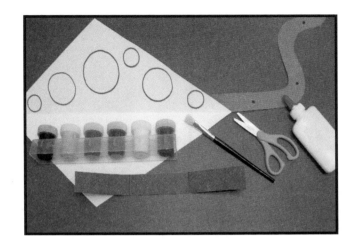

Kite Supplies:

- [ ] white diamond paper with green tail

- [ ] blue strip of paper

- [ ] paint set

- [ ] paintbrush

- [ ] scissors

- [ ] glue

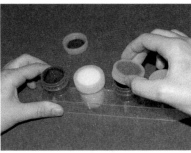

1. Take lids off green and blue paints.

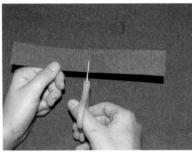

2. Paint blue and green circles on kite.

3. Fold kite.

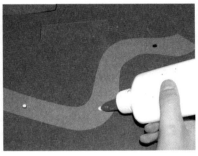

4. Cut blue strip.

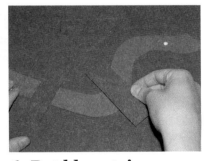

5. Put glue on dots.

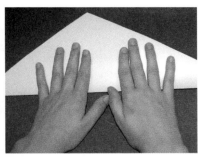

6. Put blue strips on kite tail.

7. Your kite is finished!

Ladybug

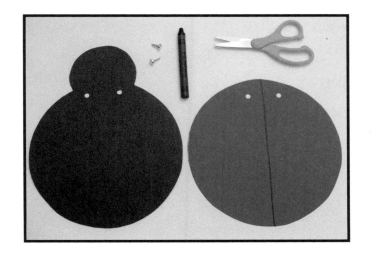

Ladybug Supplies:

- ☐ black ladybug body
- ☐ red circle
- ☐ two brads
- ☐ black crayon
- ☐ scissors

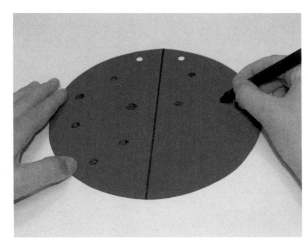

1. Draw dots on the red circle.

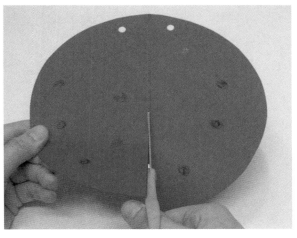

2. Cut the red circle.

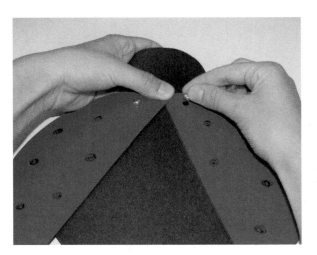

3. Put two brads into the holes.

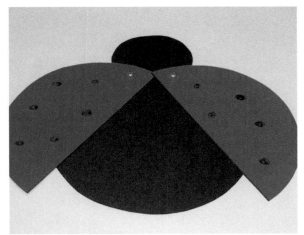

4. Did you know a ladybug is a type of beetle?

Lion

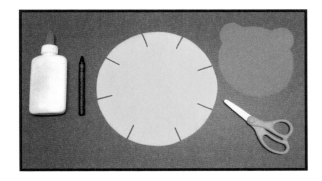

Lion Supplies:

- ☐ glue
- ☐ black crayon
- ☐ yellow circle with lines
- ☐ scissors
- ☐ orange lion head

1. Cut on lines.

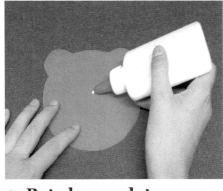

2. Put glue on dot.

3. Put lion's face on yellow circle.

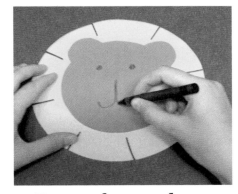

4. Draw a face on the lion.

5. Your lion is ready to rumble in the jungle!

Monster

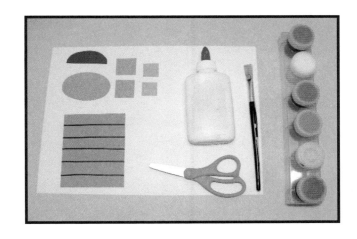

Monster Supplies:

☐ white paper

☐ monster face parts

☐ purple paper with lines

☐ paint set

☐ paintbrush

☐ scissors

☐ glue

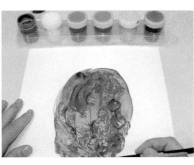

1. Paint a green oval.

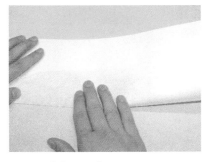

2. Fold and press your paper.

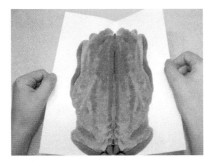

3. Open your paper.

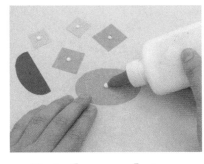

4. Put glue on dots.

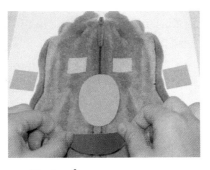

5. Put pieces on monster face.

6. Cut purple paper.

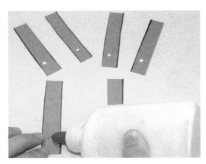

7. Put glue on dots.

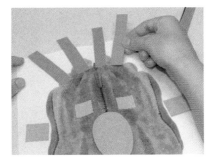

8. Put hair on the monster.

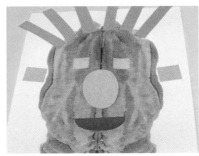

8. Go away monster!

Penguin

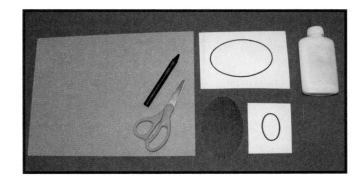

Penguin Supplies:

- [ ] blue paper
- [ ] black crayon
- [ ] scissors and glue
- [ ] big white oval and small white oval
- [ ] black oval
- [ ] two orange feet
- [ ] orange beak

1. Cut white ovals.

2. Cut black oval in half.

3. Put glue on dots.

4. Put body and head on paper.

5. Put wings on body.

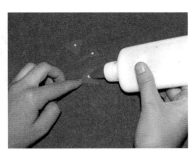

6. Put glue on dots of beak and feet.

7. Put feet and beak on the penguin.

8. Draw eyes on the penguin.

9. Penguins have webbed feet and flippers for diving and swimming!

Pizza

Pizza Supplies:

☐ orange paper

☐ brown circle

☐ red circle

☐ scissors

☐ glue

☐ pizza pieces

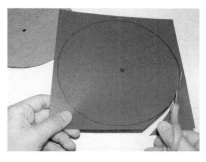

1. Cut circles for pizza.

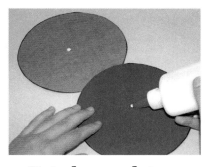

2. Put glue on dots.

3. Put brown circle on orange paper.

4. Put red circle on top of brown circle.

5. Put glue on dots.

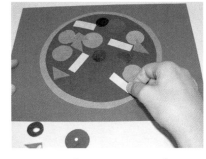

6. Put shapes on pizza.

7. Ready to eat some pizza?

Polar Bear

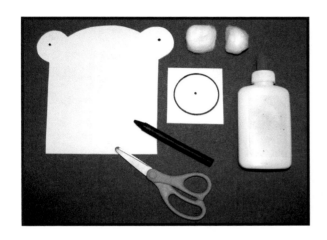

Polar Bear Supplies:

- [ ] white polar bear face
- [ ] white circle
- [ ] two cotton balls
- [ ] black crayon
- [ ] scissors
- [ ] glue

1. Cut white circle.

2. Put glue on dot.

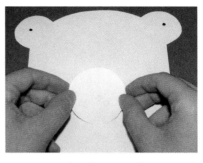

3. Put circle on face.

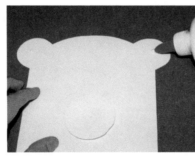

4. Put glue on dots.

5. Put cotton balls on glue.

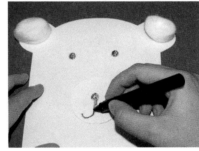

6. Draw a face on the polar bear.

7. A polar bear is a large white bear that lives in the arctic region.

Rain

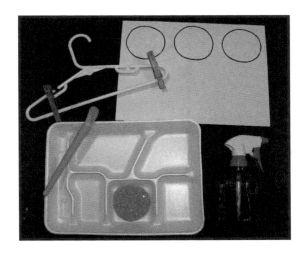

Rain Supplies:

- ☐ coat hanger
- ☐ two clothespins
- ☐ paintbrush
- ☐ blue paint
- ☐ spray bottle
- ☐ white paper

1. Paint blue in the circles.

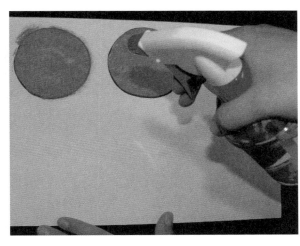

2. Spray your circles with water.

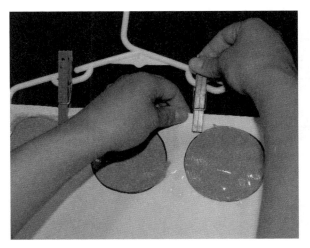

3. Clip your picture to the coat hanger with clothespins.

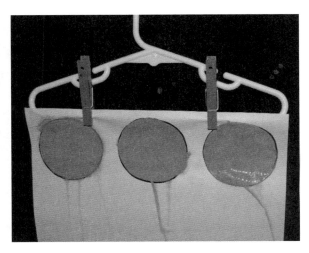

4. Let your picture drip like rain.

Scratch and Sniff

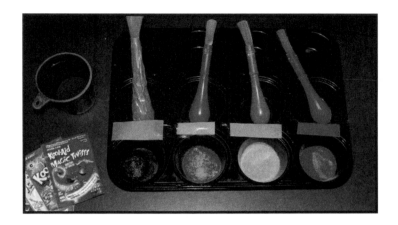

Scratch and Sniff Supplies:

☐ four colors of powdered drink mix

☐ water to mix the powdered drink

☐ paintbrushes

☐ paper

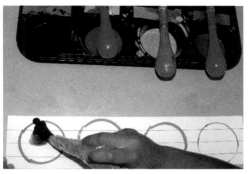

1. Paint purple drink mix in the purple circle.

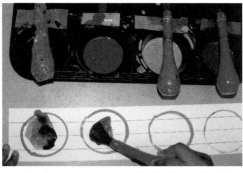

2. Paint orange drink mix in the orange circle.

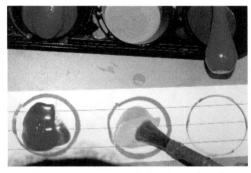

3. Paint green drink mix in the green circle.

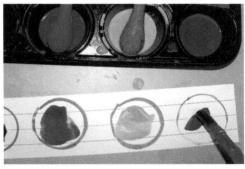

4. Paint red drink mix in the red circle.

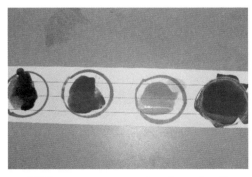

5. When your painting is dry, you can scratch and sniff it!

S'more

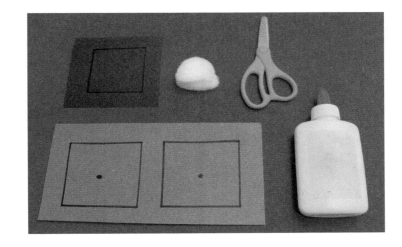

S'more Supplies:

- ☐ brown paper squares
- ☐ black paper square
- ☐ cotton ball
- ☐ scissors
- ☐ glue

1. Cut squares for s'mores.

2. Put glue on dot.

3. Put black square on top.

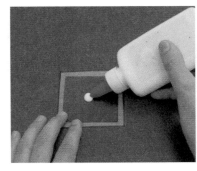

4. Put glue on dot.

5. Pull cotton ball.

6. Push cotton ball onto glue.

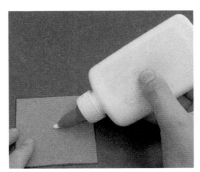

7. Put glue on dot.

8. Push square on top of cotton.

9. S'mores are a favorite snack when camping!

Snowman

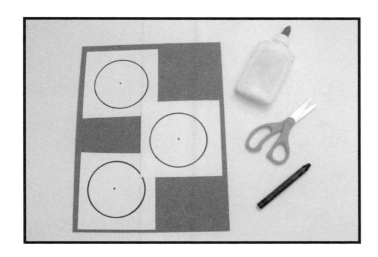

Snowman Supplies:

☐ **three white circles**

☐ **scissors**

☐ **glue**

☐ **blue paper**

☐ **black crayon**

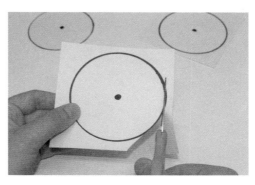

1. Cut three white circles.

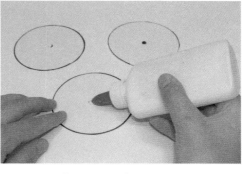

2. Put glue on dots.

3. Put circles on paper.

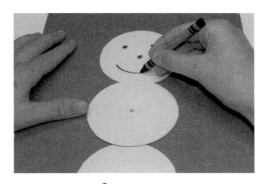

4. Draw a face on your snowman.

5. Your snowman is finished.

Snowman Fun

It's Snowing Supplies:

☐ snowman

☐ empty container

☐ shaving cream

☐ glue

1. Put shaving cream into container.

2. Put glue into container.

3. Mix shaving cream and glue.

4. Put mix around the snowman.

5. Your snowman is finished!

6. Wash your messy hands.

Sole Mate

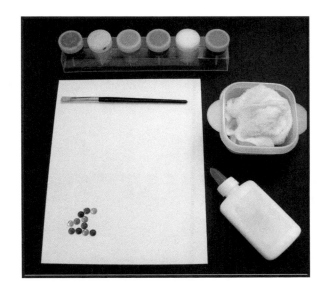

Sole Mate Supplies:

☐ white paper

☐ paintbrush and paint set

☐ ten sequins

☐ washcloth

☐ glue

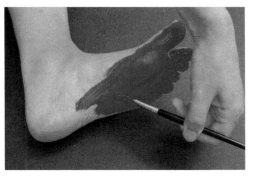

1. Paint your feet red.

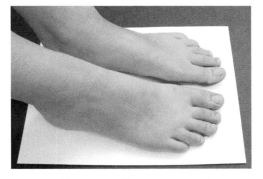

2. Push your feet onto the paper.

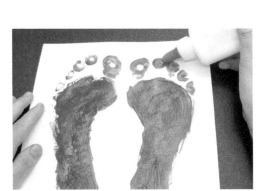

3. Put glue on toes.

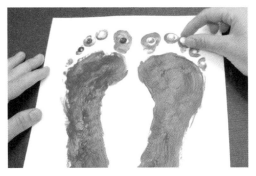

4. Put sequins on glue.

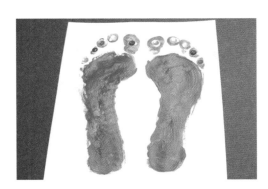

5. You are my sole mate!

Spider

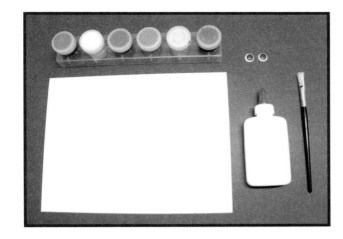

Spider Supplies:

- [ ] white paper
- [ ] paint set
- [ ] paintbrush
- [ ] two wiggle eyes
- [ ] glue

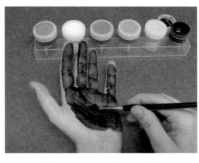

1. Paint your hand black.

2. Push your hand on the white paper.

3. Push your hand again on the paper.

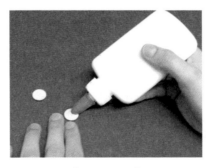

4. Put glue on the two wiggle eyes.

5. Put the wiggle eyes on the spider.

6. Your spider can spin silk thread!

7. Wash your hands.

Spring Flower

Spring Flower Supplies:

☐ blue paper

☐ yellow strip of paper

☐ green crayon

☐ glue

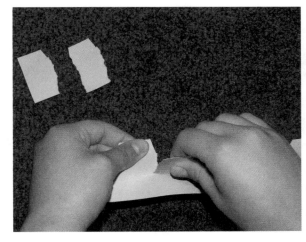

1. Tear yellow paper at notches.

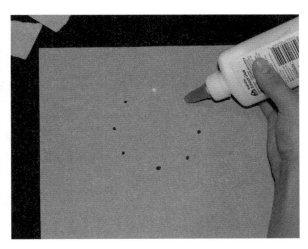

2. Put glue on dots.

3. Put yellow paper on glue.

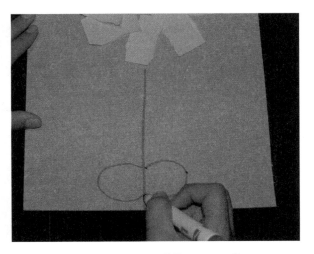

4. Draw a stem and leaves for your flower.

Tractor

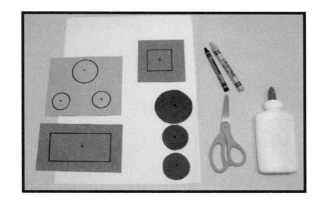

Tractor Supplies:

☐ white paper

☐ yellow and black circles

☐ green rectangle

☐ green square

☐ black and yellow crayons

☐ scissors

☐ glue

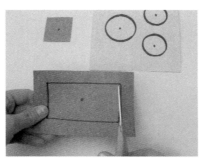

1. Cut green and yellow papers.

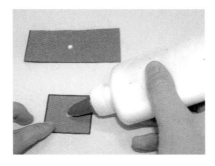

2. Put glue on green square and rectangle.

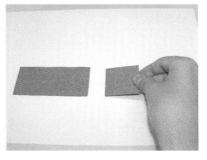

3. Put square and rectangle on the paper.

4. Put glue on black circles.

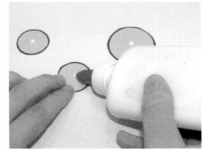

5. Put glue on yellow circles.

6. Put circles on the tractor.

7. Draw a steering wheel and a hitch.

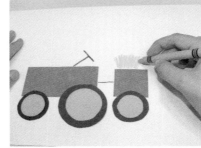

8. Draw hay in the wagon.

9. Your tractor is ready for work!

Train

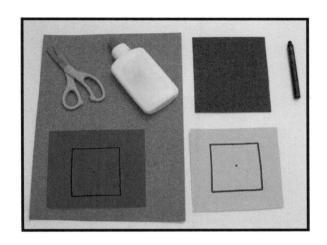

Train Supplies:

☐ green paper

☐ black engine

☐ red square

☐ yellow square

☐ black crayon

☐ scissors

☐ glue

1. Cut black engine and yellow and red squares.

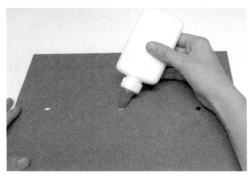

2. Put glue on dots.

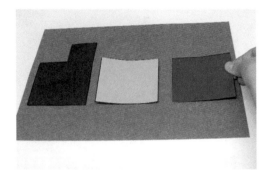

3. Put train cars on paper.

4. Draw wheels on the train.

5. Draw couplers between the train cars.

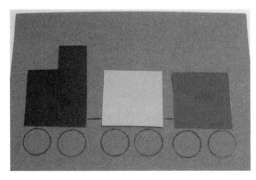

6. This is your train!

Umbrella

Umbrella Supplies:

- ☐ white paper
- ☐ black crayon
- ☐ blue crayon
- ☐ red crayon
- ☐ green crayon

1. Color green on the umbrella.

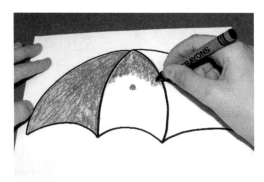

2. Color blue on the umbrella.

3. Color red on the umbrella.

4. Draw a handle for the umbrella.

5. This is your finished umbrella!

Watermelon

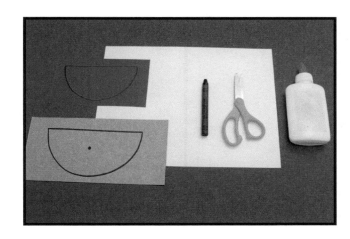

Watermelon Supplies:

☐ red and green semicircles

☐ white paper

☐ black crayon

☐ scissors

☐ glue

1. Cut green and red semicircles.

2. Put glue on dot.

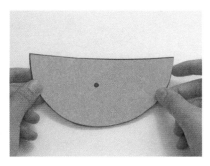

3. Put green semicircle on white paper.

4. Put glue on dot.

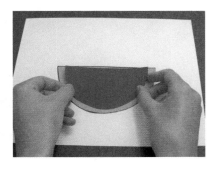

5. Put red semicircle on green paper.

6. Draw seeds on the watermelon.

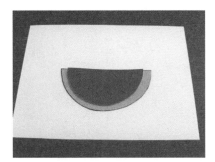

7. This is a tasty treat in the summer! Yummy watermelon!

Zebra

Zebra Supplies:

☐ white zebra

☐ black crayon

1. Draw a face on your zebra.

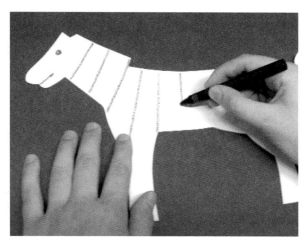

2. Draw stripes on your zebra.

3. Did you know a zebra is a swift African mammal that is related to a horse?

Zoo

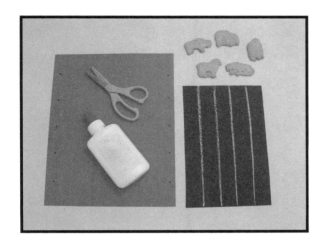

Zoo Supplies:

- ☐ black paper
- ☐ orange paper
- ☐ animal crackers
- ☐ scissors
- ☐ glue

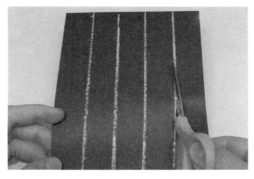

1. Cut lines on black paper.

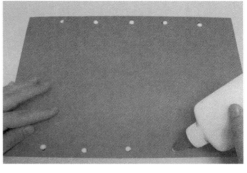

2. Put glue on dots.

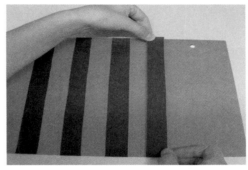

3. Put black strips of paper on the orange paper.

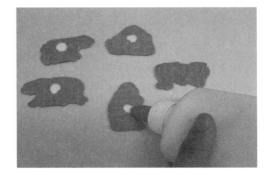

4. Put glue on animal crackers.

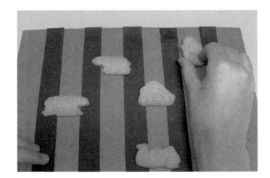

5. Put the animal crackers in the cage.

6. Your zoo cage is finished!

Resources

Development of Hand Skills in the Child.
Jane Case-Smith, Charlane Pehoski (1992).
Bethesda, Maryland: American Occupational Therapy Association.

Hand Function in the Child: Foundations for Remediation.
Anne Henderson, Charlane Pehoski (2005).
St. Louis, Missouri: Mosby, Inc.

Inclusive Programming for Elementary Students with Autism.
Sheila Wagner (1998).
Arlington, Texas: Future Horizons, Inc.

The Out-of-Sync Child: Recognizing and Coping with Sensory Processing Disorder, Revised Edition.
Carol Stock Kranowitz (2006).
New York, New York: Perigee Books.

SenseAbilities: Understanding Sensory Integration.
Maryann Colby Trott, Marci K. Laurel, Susan L. Windeck (1993).
Tucson, Arizona: Therapy Skill Builders.

Tasks Galore book series.
Laurie Eckenrode, Pat Fennell, Kathy Hearsey (2003, 2004, 2005).
Raleigh, North Carolina: Tasks Galore Publishing, Inc.

The TEACCH Approach to Autism Spectrum Disorders.
Gary B. Mesibov, Victoria Shea, Eric Schlopler (2005).
New York, New York: Kluwer Academic/Plenum Publishers.

Visual Strategies for Improving Communication: Practical Supports for School and Home.
Linda A. Hodgdon (1995).
Troy, Michigan: Quirk Roberts Publishing.